My Claws Are Large and Curved

by Jessica Rudolph

Consultants:
Christopher Kuhar, PhD
Executive Director
Cleveland Metroparks Zoo
Cleveland, Ohio

Kimberly Brenneman, PhD
National Institute for Early Education Research
Rutgers University
New Brunswick, New Jersey

BEARPORT PUBLISHING

New York, New York

Credits

Cover, © steve estvanik/Shutterstock; 4–5, © Anna Yu/Alamy; 6–7, © iStockphoto/Thinkstock; 8–9, © Jaromir Cihak/Dreamstime.com; 10–11, © Stephen Frink Collection/Alamy; 12–13, © dbimages/Alamy; 14–15, © Anna Yu/Alamy; 16–17, © iStockphoto/Thinkstock; 18–19, © Barry Kusuma/Getty; 20–21, © Barry Kusuma/Getty; 22, © Michael Pitts/naturepl.com; 23, © Ekaterina V. Borisova/Shutterstock; 24, © Levent Konuk/Shutterstock.

Publisher: Kenn Goin
Creative Director: Spencer Brinker
Design: Debrah Kaiser
Photo Researcher: Michael Win

Library of Congress Cataloging-in-Publication Data

Rudolph, Jessica.
  My claws are large and curved / by Jessica Rudolph.
      pages cm. — (Zoo clues)
  Includes bibliographical references and index.
  Audience: Ages 5–8.
  ISBN-13: 978-1-62724-114-4 (library binding)
  ISBN-10: 1-62724-114-0 (library binding)
  1. Komodo dragon—Juvenile literature. I. Title.
  QL666.L29R83 2014
  597.95'968—dc23

                          2013036946

For more information, write to Bearport Publishing Company, Inc., 45 West 21st Street, Suite 3B, New York, New York 10010. Printed in the United States of America.

10 9 8 7 6 5 4 3 2 1

Contents

What Am I?

Look at my tongue.

4

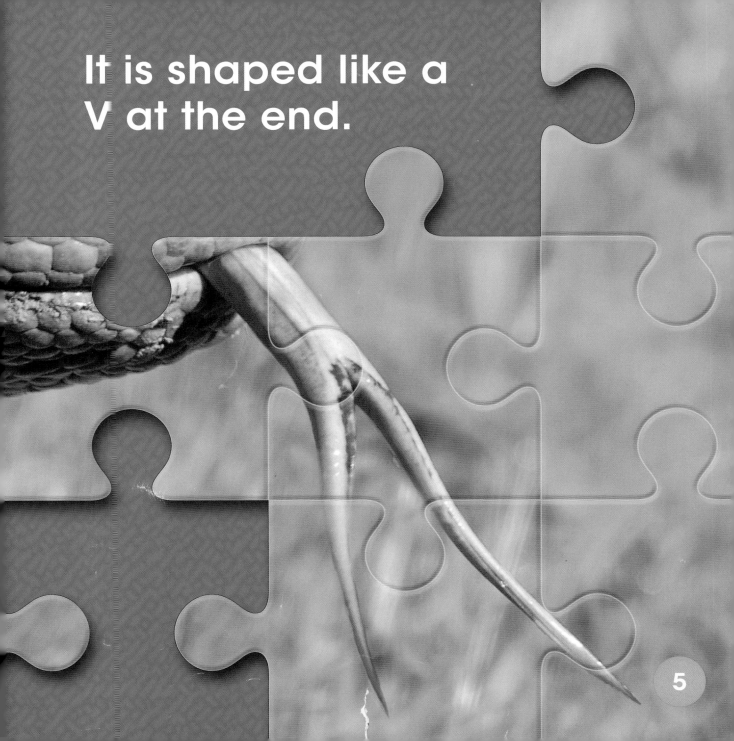

It is shaped like a
V at the end.

5

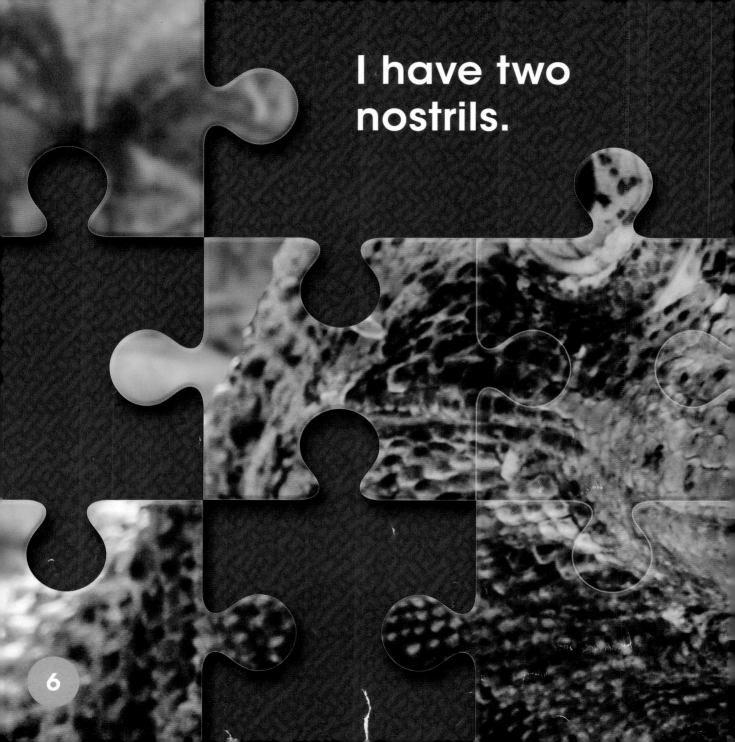

I have two nostrils.

6

They are big
and round.

My tail is long
and brown.

8

9

My legs are short and strong.

I have four feet.

12

Each foot has large, curved claws.

My mouth is
wide and pink.

14

15

I have
rough skin.

16

It is scaly.

What am I?

Let's find out!

19

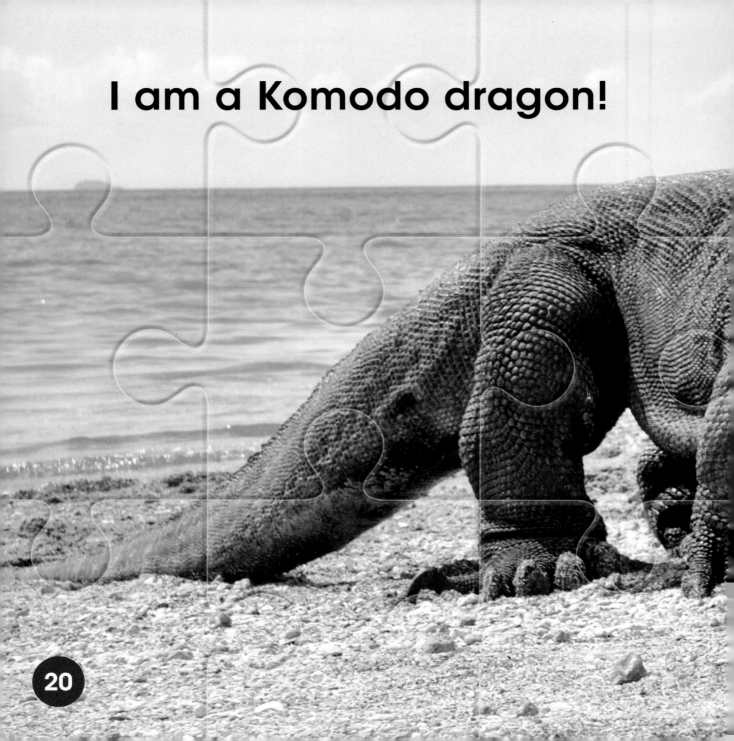

I am a Komodo dragon!

Animal Facts

Komodo dragons are lizards. All lizards belong to a group of animals called reptiles. Like almost all reptiles, Komodo dragons lay eggs instead of giving birth to live young. Their bodies are also covered with scales.

More Komodo Dragon Facts

Food:	Deer, pigs, water buffalo, rodents, and snakes
Size:	10 feet (3 m) long, including the tail
Weight:	Up to 300 pounds (136 kg)
Life Span:	Up to 30 years in the wild
Cool Fact:	A Komodo dragon uses its tongue to smell food that is up to three miles (4.8 km) away.

Adult Komodo Dragon Size

Where Do I Live?

Komodo dragons live on a few islands in Southeast Asia. They are found in forests and grasslands.

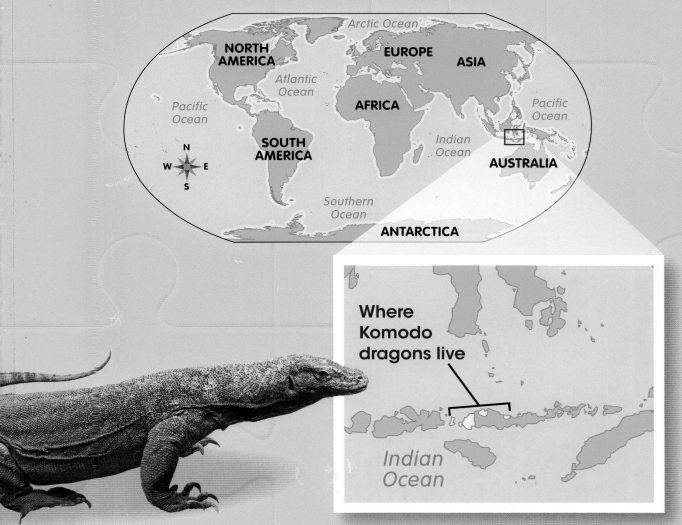

Where Komodo dragons live

Index

Read More

Bodden, Valerie. *Komodo Dragons (Amazing Animals).* Mankato, MN: Creative (2014).

Lunis, Natalie. *Komodo Dragon: The World's Biggest Lizard (SuperSized!).* New York: Bearport (2007).

Learn More Online

To learn more about Komodo dragons, visit **www.bearportpublishing.com/ZooClues**

About the Author

Jessica Rudolph lives in Connecticut. She has edited and written many books about history, science, and nature for children.